# WORDS GAMES WITH ENGLISH PLUS

**Deirdre Howard-Williams**

**and Cynthia Herd**

HEINEMANN

# Heinemann Games Series

## Titles in this series include:

**Word Games with English 1**  Deirdre Howard-Williams & Cynthia Herd  0 435 28380 4
**Word Games with English 2**  Deirdre Howard-Williams & Cynthia Herd  0 435 28381 2
**Word Games with English 3**  Deirdre Howard-Williams & Cynthia Herd  0 435 28382 0
**Word Games with English Plus**  Deirdre Howard-Williams & Cynthia Herd  0 435 28379 0

**Play Games With English Book 1**  Colin Granger  0 435 28060 0
Teacher's Book 1  0 435 28061 9
**Play Games With English Book 2**  Colin Granger  0 435 28062 7
Teacher's Book 2  0 435 28063 5

**English Puzzles 1**  Doug Case  0 435 28280 8
**English Puzzles 2**  Doug Case  0 435 28281 6

Heinemann International
a division of Heinemann Educational Books Ltd
Halley Court, Jordan Hill, Oxford OX2 8EJ

OXFORD  LONDON  EDINBURGH  MADRID  ATHENS  BOLOGNA
MELBOURNE  SYDNEY  AUCKLAND  IBADAN  NAIROBI  GABORONE  HARARE
KINGSTON  PORTSMOUTH (NH)  SINGAPORE

ISBN 0 435 28379 0

*Illustrated by*
Caroline Ewen pp 3, 6, 7, 9, 10, 11, 12, 14, 18, 21, 26, 30, 32, 36, 37, 40, 43
Joanna Isles pp 24, 38, 39   Kim Lane pp 1, 4, 5, 8, 17, 25, 27, 34, 35, 44, 45
Brian Whitehead pp 2, 12, 13, 15, 19, 23, 31, 37, 41, 46

The road signs on page 31 are reproduced from *The Highway Code* with the permission
of the Controller of Her Majesty's Stationery Office

Set in Helvetica

Printed and bound in Great Britain by
Thomson Litho Ltd, East Kilbride, Scotland

90  91  92  93  94  10  9  8  7  6  5  4  3  2

# About this book

- *Word Games With English Plus* is the fourth book in the *Word Games With English* series. It is designed to stimulate upper-intermediate learners to practise, activate and extend their English vocabulary.

## Pedagogical Basis

- *Word Games With English Plus* corresponds to the standard demanded for the University of Cambridge First Certificate in English, where students are expected to have a good level of general English vocabulary in the 4000 to 5000 word range.

- The words have been taken from the *Cambridge English Lexicon* (R. Hindmarsh) at levels 4 and 5, from First Certificate in English examination papers and from the most widely-used English as a Foreign Language textbooks. Extensive use has been made of authentic materials, such as travel brochures, information booklets and newspapers, and patterns of use have been checked in a wide variety of modern dictionaries.

- *Word Games With English Plus* can be used to complement any course at this level, filling lexical gaps and providing further practice.

- Learners are also prepared for the type of vocabulary and the kind of language manipulation that are required for the First Certificate in English examination.

## Presentation

- The vocabulary illustrates a wide variety of topic areas and semantic fields: travel and holidays, the media, leisure activities, tools and appliances, finance etc.

- The games develop an awareness of different language forms: phrasal verbs, compounds, prefixes and suffixes, homonyms, homophones etc.

- Special practice has been given in collocation, lexical choice and appropriacy as these are a major source of error at this level.

- There is a wide variety of activities: matching, selecting, labelling, cloze testing etc to encourage students to think in English.

- The book is suitable for adults and teenagers, for individual or group work, and for varied further exploitation by the teacher, who can use it in class or for homework.

- There is a full answer key and word list , enabling the book to be used for self-study and revision.

# How to use this book

To do all the games in this book, you will have to use the English words you know and learn many more. Read the instructions carefully before you start each game. Study the example and make sure you understand what you have to do — matching words, inserting words into spaces, finding the missing words etc.

Write your answers in the book if there is room or on a piece of paper. Some of the games may take quite a long time, so do not give up too easily. Try to find the answers you do not know by looking at the context, the other words in the game and the letters needed. The Word List at the back of the book contains all the words used in the games and is there to help you. Use it to give you ideas and guide you towards the correct solution.

When you have done all you can, refer to the answer key to check and correct your work. Keep the book as a record when it is completed and as a check list of words you should know.

And you can always rub out the answers and start again!

# CONTENTS

To Miranda Belle Argenson and Betty Goodall Stuart

# Food for Thought

A busy restaurant serves the following: MEAT, FISH, VEGETABLE CURRY, SAUCES, BREAD, FRUIT, WINE and COFFEE.
If you heard these complaints from diners, what would they be talking about?

For example:
1 BREAD

Now choose from the adjectives below to describe the following in different ways:
(some of the adjectives can be used more than once)

For example:

| a cup of tea | a type of cheese | a glass of lemonade |
|---|---|---|
| 1 strong | 1 _____ | 1 _____ |
| 2 milky | 2 _____ | 2 _____ |
| 3 _____ | 3 _____ | 3 _____ |
| 4 _____ | 4 _____ | 4 _____ |
| 5 _____ | 5 _____ | 5 _____ |
| 6 _____ | 6 _____ | 6 _____ |

(strong)    ripe    mild    iced    sweet    tasty    tough    weak
sparkling    crumbly    refreshing    hard    dry    still    fizzy    (milky)

# Four of a Kind

Follow the zigzag down and find the noun which can go with all 4 words.

*For example:* 1 box

(4 kinds of box : signal box, window box, fuse box and witness box)

| | | | | |
|---|---|---|---|---|
| signal / window / fuse / witness | green / light / council / public | sewing / fruit / slot / vending | dining / racing / sports / cable | surf / diving / notice / black |
| **1** box | **2** | **3** | **4** | **5** |
| wall / exam / toilet / wrapping | Christmas / credit / identity / membership | reading / sun / opera / dark | class / spare / changing / store | sleeping / paper / carrier / shoulder |
| **6** | **7** | **8** | **9** | **10** |
| over / under / mink / rain | flower / tea / chimney / jack | clothes / dotted / yellow / assembly | race / rocking / sea / cart | cheque / exercise / phone / phrase |
| **11** | **12** | **13** | **14** | **15** |
| search / political / dinner / birthday | maiden / family / brand / pet | card / kitchen / billiard / bedside | cigarette / book / dead / loose | correspondence / race / main / golf |
| **16** | **17** | **18** | **19** | **20** |

Heinemann International

# Word Perfect

These pairs of words are often confused. Look at the pictures and choose the correct word.

For example:

1. date/appointment
2. lose/loose
3. advertisement/warning
4. line/row
5. souvenir/memory
6. employee/employer
7. pass/take
8. advice/information
9. interruption/interval
10. win/earn
11. angel/angle
12. sensitive/sensible
13. melt/dissolve
14. economic/economical
15. clothes/cloths
16. quite/quiet

Now use 4 of the incorrect words to describe the 4 pictures below.

17. 18. 19. 20.

# What's on

On these T.V. screens, you can see excerpts from an evening's viewing on several different channels. The titles of the programmes watched by Adrian and by Elizabeth will enable you to identify what each of them saw. Match the screens to the titles then number the screens accordingly. Then look at the group of words on the page opposite. All these words are connected with T.V.

For example:

                    Heinemann International

# TV Tonight?

**ADRIAN** watched the following programmes:   **1** The World Tonight: An Up-to-the-Minute Report   **2** Is it Really a Bargain? Two Teams of Antiques Experts Compete. **3** Top of the Pops–This Week's Best-Selling Singles.   **4** Use Your Vote Wisely. A Message from the Leader of the Opposition.   **5** Wish on a Star: A Galaxy of Top Entertainers.   **6** The Masked Raiders' Revenge: Will give you Nightmares! Don't watch alone!

**ELIZABETH** watched the following programmes:   **7** The Open University Foundation Course.   **8** Athletics: Highlights from the Qualifying Rounds.   **9** Never a Dull Moment with Desmond the Duck: Fun for Young and Old.   **10** The European Economic Community: A Closer Look.   **11** I.Q. Challenge: Beat the Clock to Win the Jackpot.   **12** Evening Worship: Prayers and Thanksgiving.

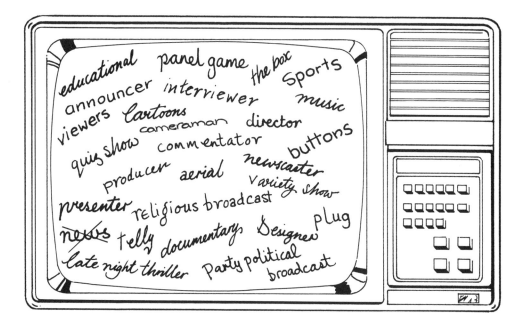

First cross out the 12 words or expressions which describe the 12 different types of programme you have just identified on the previous page. Then cross out:

**5** people who appear on the screen
**4** people who work behind the scenes
**3** parts of a television
**2** slang words for television
**1** word for those who watch

# Leisure & Pleasure

Take 1 letter from each word in the lists below to find 12 popular leisure activities and interests that people enjoy in their spare time. The words in the lists are all connected to each activity.

The same 12 words are also hidden in the word square below. Use this to give you ideas and to check your answers.

For example:

**1** socks **needles** cardigan thread **stitch** plain pattern gloves _knitting_

**2** valuable china furniture rarity quality beauty objects shops _ _ _ _ _ _ _ _

**3** shape decoration earthenware craft wheel fire clay _ _ _ _ _ _ _

**4** pointed aim score throw pubs _ _ _ _ _

**5** championship check mate bishop castle _ _ _ _ _

**6** company tame cats stroke _ _ _ _

**7** director critics curtain amateur applause _ _ _ _ _

**8** make objects display miniature collect scale _ _ _ _ _ _

**9** clubs cards diamonds spades game hearts _ _ _ _ _ _

**10** fabrics magazines style clothing designers models changes _ _ _ _ _ _ _

**11** recipe oven boil cake stove apron electricity _ _ _ _ _ _ _

**12** stamina strength rhythm oxygen body fit exercise gym _ _ _ _ _ _ _

The words are horizontal ⬭, vertical ◖, or diagonal ⬭

For example:

| a | e | r | o | b | i | c | s | l | u | i |
|---|---|---|---|---|---|---|---|---|---|---|
| w | l | a | k | m | o | d | e | l | s | g |
| u | d | o | n | g | h | c | h | e | s | s |
| f | e | h | i | d | o | f | u | t | c | y |
| a | r | d | t | a | m | q | a | d | r | b |
| s | t | r | t | r | i | x | t | e | l | r |
| h | s | a | i | t | u | s | k | y | p | i |
| i | b | m | n | s | n | o | l | j | e | d |
| o | r | a | g | e | o | z | d | s | t | g |
| n | t | q | h | c | s | a | u | p | s | e |
| y | d | e | t | p | o | t | t | e | r | y |

                    Heinemann International

# Treasure Hunt

Treasure is buried somewhere in this garden. It is NOT buried in any of the squares containing the things below (1–15). Write the letter of each of these squares in the boxes and then cross them out on the picture. This will tell you what the treasure is and you'll find it in the square that is left.

For example:

1 stable

2 kennel

3 flower beds

4 barn

5 bushes

6 birdbath

7 toolshed

8 rake

9 well

10 haystack

11 pond

12 greenhouse

13 it's not in a square along the path

14 or beside the fence

15 and it's not on or under the benches

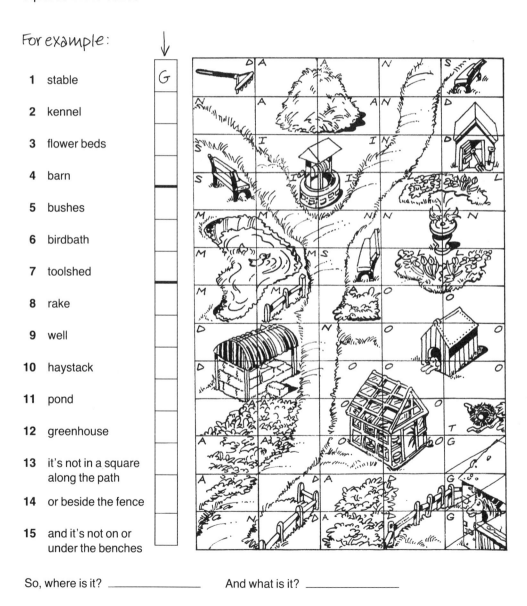

So, where is it? _____     And what is it? _____

# DOMINOES 1

Play a game of dominoes with words instead of numbers to find 17 objects from a kitchen. If you play correctly you'll use all the dominoes.

For example:

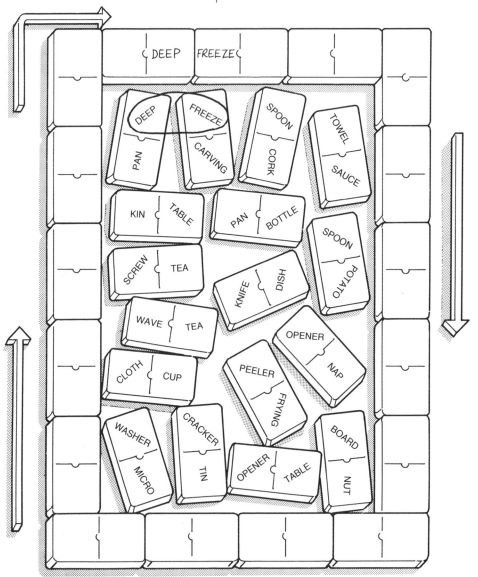

© Howard-Williams/Herd 1989                    Heinemann International

# The Animal Kingdom

Look at all the living creatures and classify them according to one of their features. The letter spaces and their position will help you. Then match the animals' names with the pictures.

For example:

V = 1 | C | R | A | B
N = 2 | L | E | O | P | A | R | D
3 | | A
4 | | W

5 | P
6 | | A
7 | W

8 | F
9 | | U
10 | | R

11 | | T
12 | | A
13 | | I
14 | | L

15 | | H
16 | | O
17 | | R
18 | | N

19 | W
20
21 | | N
22 | | G

23 | H
24 | O
25 | O
26 | F

# *Guilty or*

All the answers to this puzzle are connected with crime and justice. Find each word by adding (when you see the symbol +) and taking away (when you see the symbol −) the letters shown beside each picture. Occasionally you may have to change the letter order as well.

For example : the answer to number 1 is jail ( 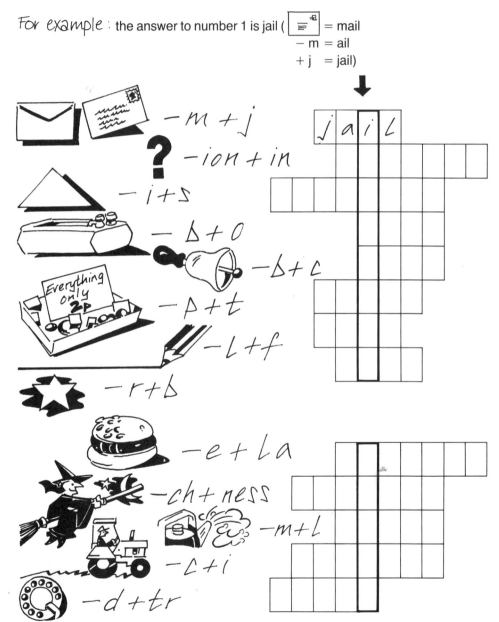 = mail
− m = ail
+ j = jail)

   Heinemann International

# Not Guilty

If all your answers are correct, you will be able to read a belief that is at the heart of the British legal system: _____ _____ _____ _____

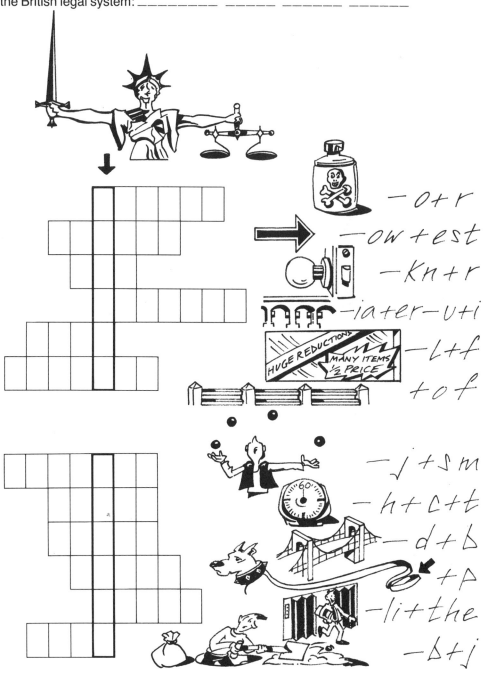

$-o+r$

$-ow+est$

$-kn+r$

$-ia+er-u+i$

$-L+f$

$+o f$

$-j+sm$

$-h+c+t$

$-d+b$

$+A$

$-li+the$

$-b+j$

# GLIDOGRAM 1

Complete the Glidogram by looking at the clues. The first 12 words all contain the letters **OR** and the second 12 the letters **ENT** (3 at the beginning of the word, 4 in the middle of the word and 5 at the end of the word each time).

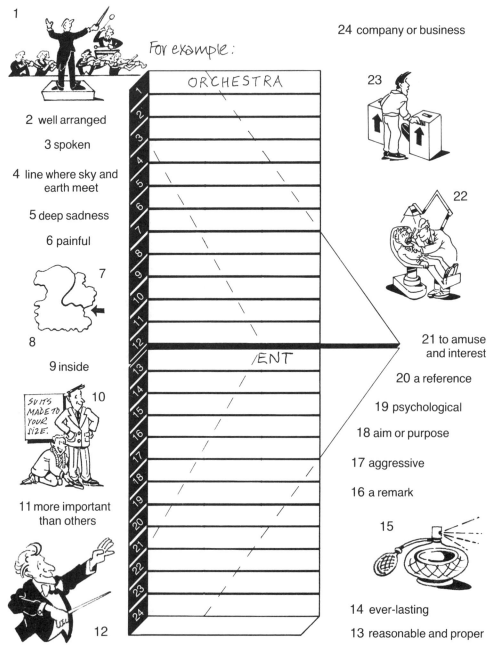

1

24 company or business

23

22

21 to amuse and interest

20 a reference

19 psychological

18 aim or purpose

17 aggressive

16 a remark

15

14 ever-lasting

13 reasonable and proper

2 well arranged

3 spoken

4 line where sky and earth meet

5 deep sadness

6 painful

7

8

9 inside

10

SUITS MADE TO YOUR SIZE.

11 more important than others

12

For example:

ORCHESTRA

/ENT

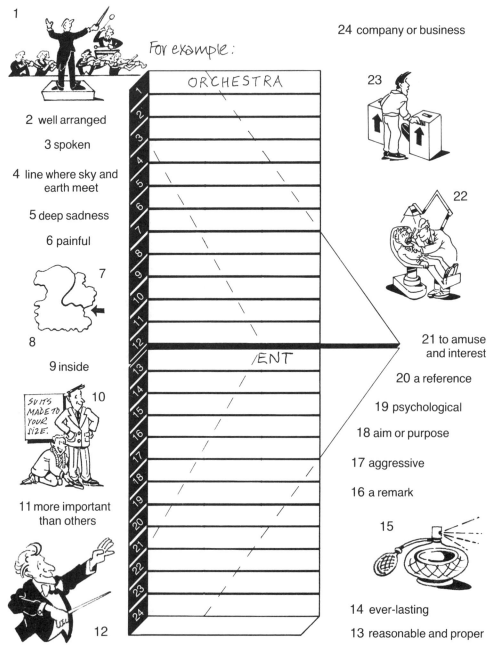

# The Good Companions

Certain adjectives are only used with certain nouns. For each of the adjectives below choose the 3 nouns it can be used with.

**1** high    **2** expensive    **3** powerful    **4** remote    **5** aggressive
**6** dry    **7** bright    **8** tidy    **9** steady    **10** false    **11** dull
**12** plain    **13** deep    **14** heavy

*For example : 1 high = G*

(We talk about a *high temperature, a high price* and *a high standard.*)

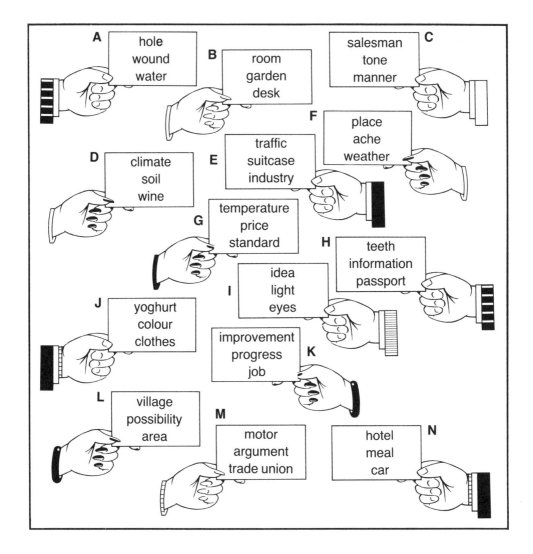

A — hole / wound / water
B — room / garden / desk
C — salesman / tone / manner
D — climate / soil / wine
E — traffic / suitcase / industry
F — place / ache / weather
G — temperature / price / standard
H — teeth / information / passport
I — idea / light / eyes
J — yoghurt / colour / clothes
K — improvement / progress / job
L — village / possibility / area
M — motor / argument / trade union
N — hotel / meal / car

# Family Gatherings

In these groups of 7 words, circle the word which includes the others and cross out the word which does not belong to the same family.

For example : **1** circle (insect) as ant, fly, butterfly, beetle and bee are all insects and cross out snail as a snail is not an insect.

1   ant   fly   (insect)   butterfly   beetle   bee   ~~snail~~

2   alligator   reptile   snake   frog   tortoise   lizard   crocodile

3   trout   whale   salmon   cod   tuna   fish

4   acrylic   ribbon   velvet   silk   linen   material   nylon

5   steamer   yacht   ferry   ship   liner   tanker   raft

6   chestnut   log   oak   plane   tree   pine   fir

7   plum   melon   tomato   seed   grape   fruit   peach

8   custard   dessert   ice-cream   jelly   porridge   tart   trifle

9   island   Ireland   America   Malta   Cyprus   Iceland   Australia

10   sympathy   envy   honesty   virtue   bravery   kindness   generosity

11   launch   cab   tandem   sledge   coach   vehicle   tram

12   china   saucer   vase   napkin   jug   dish   teapot

13   thought   sight   touch   sense   hearing   smell   taste

14   greed   hatred   jealousy   gluttony   vice   anger   patience

15   coal   tin   metal   steel   copper   lead   iron

      Heinemann International

# WORDBOARD 1

The words you are looking for have 2 meanings. You have the first letter and one of the meanings given on the wordboard. Complete the word and select another completely different definition from those given below.

For example :

**1**

M _I_ _N_ _D_

TO LOOK AFTER

TO OBJECT TO

**2**

C _ _ _ _

A SPORTS TRAINER

**3**

F _ _ _ _

AN EXHIBITION

**4**

S _ _ _ _ _ _

A PERIOD iN A DEVELOPMENT

**5**

S _ _ _ _ _ _

A POLITICAL COMMUNITY

**6**

H _ _ _

WITH GREAT ENERGY

**7**

F _ _ _ _

DELICATE

**8**

P _ _ _ _ _ _ _

A SICK PERSON

**9**

H _ _ _ _

A POINTER ON A CLOCK

**10**

S _ _ _ _ _

NOT SPARKLING

**11**

S _ _ _ _ _

A SMALL STALL

**12**

C _ _ _ _

A MEDICAL PROBLEM

CALM    QUIET    TO PASS    A PENALTY    BLONDE
1 (TO LOOK AFTER)    A PLATFORM IN A THEATRE
TO EXPRESS IN WORDS    TO ENDURE    AN EXAMPLE
SEVERELY    A CARRIAGE

# SUPER

It's Ruben's first day working for SUPER TRIPS Travel Agency. In order to answer the points raised in this letter from a disatisfied customer, which sections of the SUPER TRIPS FAIR TRADING AGREEMENT does he need to consult?

For example:

> See No.5 complaints

... the swimming pool was terribly dirty and I slipped on the steps and now can't use my right thumb. The return flight was changed at the last minute, so I missed my connection and you gave me an aisle seat when I wanted to be beside the window. And when I opened my case at home, all my glass souvenirs were broken ...

Heinemann International

# TRIPS

In the afternoon, he has to deal with lots of different queries. Where will he find the answers?

For example: A = 4 and 23 Cancellation

# Do-it-yourself

Sam is a good handyman and has just made this kitchen cabinet for his new flat. Can you complete the word grid with the names of all the materials and tools he used. Follow the numbers.

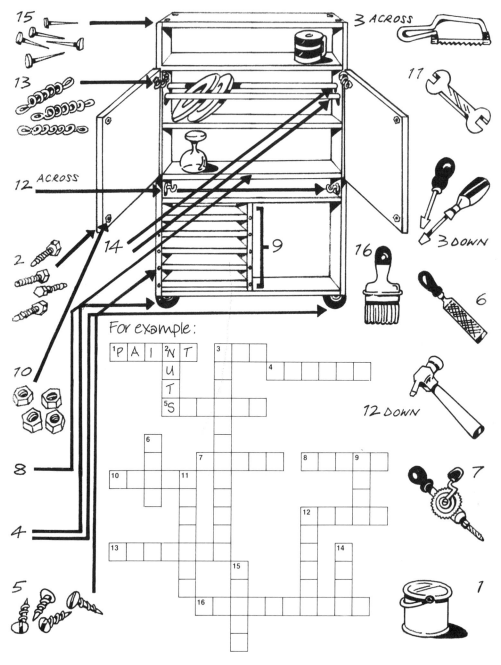

For example:

| ¹P | A | I | ²N | T |
|----|---|---|----|---|
|    |   |   | U  |   |
|    |   |   | T  |   |
|    |   |   | ⁵S |   |

# Sy-lla-ble search

There are 15 nouns in this honeycomb, divided into syllables. Join the syllables by tracing through them to find the answers to the questions. The first syllable of each word is marked in **bold**.

For example:
1 = RE LATION SHIP

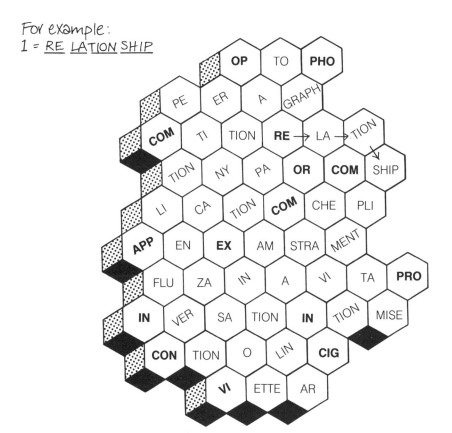

1 What can you establish and break off?
2 What can you light and put out?
3 What can you sit and get through?
4 What can you pay or accept?
5 What can you perform or recover from?
6 What can you enter and win?
7 What can you accept or turn down?
8 What can you make or break?
9 What can you take and develop?
10 What can you conduct and play in?
11 What can you put in and have rejected?
12 What can you catch and get over?
13 What can you hold or interrupt?
14 What can you practise and tune?
15 What can you set up or take over?

# Small Ads

Look at these 12 short advertisements from the small ads. section of a local newspaper. A new secretary typed them and made some mistakes! Now the boss has asked you to correct them. First circle the word that is out of place in the ad. Then put each word with its correct small ad. in the space provided.

---

*For example:*

1 **COOKER**, excellent condition, 4 hot plates, _grill_ timer, (sunroof.)

2 **MUSIC CENTRE**, dual cassette, turntable, F.M. radio, pump, compact disc player _____.

3 **INSTANTAMATIC CAMERA**, _____, case, filters, sideboard, prints ready in minutes.

4 **NATURAL FARM PRODUCE**, _____, home-grown fruit and vegetables, plastering, cheese, oak smoked salmon, duck eggs, animals and fat-free yoghurt.

5 **JUST PASSED YOUR DRIVING TEST**? Be different! Buy a Morris Minor 1954! Tax and M.O.T. _____, labels, beige bodywork, fog lights. Two careful owners. Bargain.

6 **THE GARDEN CENTRE – ANNUAL SALE**. Soil, pot plants,_____, tele-lens, exotic species, also tools, spades and forks.

7 **DINING SUITE**, 4 high-backed chairs, playpens, drinks cabinet, extending oval table, _____.

8 **ROOFING AND PROPERTY MAINTENANCE**. Re-tiling, chimney servicing, rubbish cleared, _____, window cleaning, grill, pipes.

9 **BICYCLE**, ladies, basket, pedigree, stainless steel frame, child's seat, _____.

10 **EVERYTHING TO WELCOME THE NEW MEMBER OF THE FAMILY**: prams, folding pushchairs, carry cots, _____, high chairs, loudspeakers, teddybears and other soft toys.

11 **GOOD HOME WANTED** for 8 year-old, black Collie bitch. Organic, _____, vaccinated. Due to owner's illness.

12 **OFFICE EQUIPMENT AND STATIONERY: CLOSING DOWN SALE**. Everything must go. Hundreds of bargains. Appointment diaries, note pads, _____, bulbs, typewriter ribbons, calculators.

---

The details below were left out completely. Decide which small ad. they belong to and number them accordingly.

| | | |
|---|---|---|
| solid oak | stereo headphones | free estimates |
| free range | 3-speed | low mileage |
| auto-focus | filing cabinets | dolls |
| lovely temperament | self-cleaning oven (1) | rakes |

    Heinemann International

# Verb Vertigo 1

Do phrasal verbs make you dizzy? Climb the ladder step by step. The two verbs share the same three prepositions or adverbs. The words and pictures beside each group will help you to find the answers.

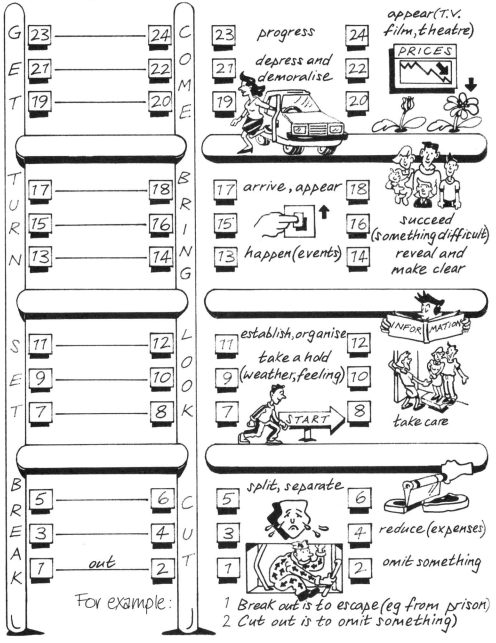

**G E T** 23 — 24 **C O M E**
27 — 22
19 — 20

**T U R N** 17 — 18 **B R I N G**
15 — 16
13 — 14

**S E T** 11 — 12 **L O O K**
9 — 10
7 — 8

**B R E A K** 5 — 6 **C U T**
3 — 4
1 — out — 2

23 progress — 24 appear (T.V. film, theatre)
27 depress and demoralise — 22 PRICES
19 — 20

17 arrive, appear — 18
15 — 16 succeed (something difficult)
13 happen (events) — 14 reveal and make clear

11 establish, organise — 12 INFORMATION
9 take a hold (weather, feeling) — 10
7 START — 8 take care

5 split, separate — 6
3 — 4 reduce (expenses)
1 — 2 omit something

For example:

1 Break out is to escape (eg from prison)
2 Cut out is to omit something)

# Gatwick

Gatwick Airport, 35 miles south of London, is the fourth largest in the world. To help you to be able to find your way around an international airport make sure you can put the following words and expressions into 6 groups.

*For example*: wheelchair users = 6 (facilities at the airport)

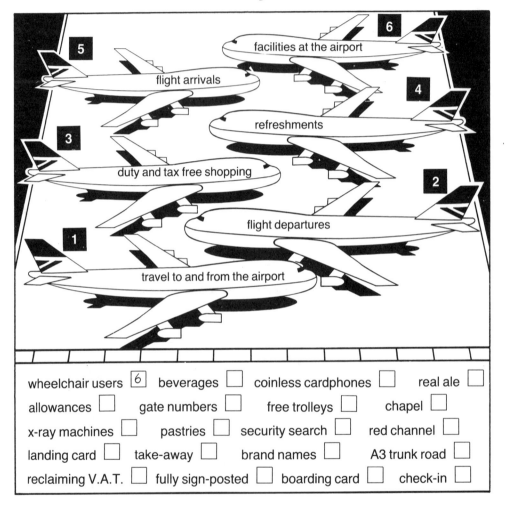

wheelchair users 6   beverages ☐   coinless cardphones ☐   real ale ☐

allowances ☐   gate numbers ☐   free trolleys ☐   chapel ☐

x-ray machines ☐   pastries ☐   security search ☐   red channel ☐

landing card ☐   take-away ☐   brand names ☐   A3 trunk road ☐

reclaiming V.A.T. ☐   fully sign-posted ☐   boarding card ☐   check-in ☐

The police are waiting on the second floor of Gatwick Airport terminal for Mr X who is strongly suspected of carrying a parcel containing secret documents. First read the policeman's notes on the page opposite and trace Mr X's route on the plan.
When the police stopped Mr X the parcel he was carrying was empty. So what do you think happened to the secret documents? Work it out alone or with a partner, then compare your ideas with the solution in the answers.

# Airport

Gatwick Airport: Notes on suspect's movements

1. Suspect arrives through Green Channel with luggage.
2. Makes hotel booking for one night.
3. Attempts to purchase stamps, but the machine seems out of order.
4. Tries to force machine with help of passer-by heading for post office counter.
5. Mail collected by postman.
6. Suspect proceeds to coach park — in error?
7. Doubles back to railway entrance.
8. Parcel seized and opened. Empty!

## INTERNATIONAL FLIGHT ARRIVALS
### 2nd FLOOR OF TERMINAL

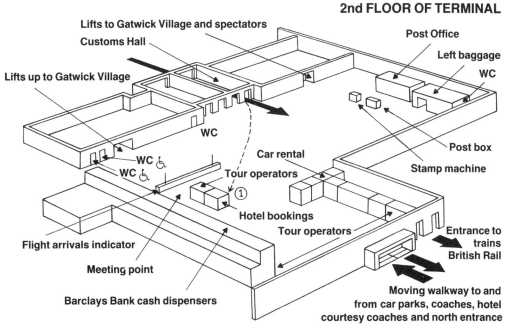

Lifts to Gatwick Village and spectators

Customs Hall

Lifts up to Gatwick Village

Post Office

Left baggage

WC

WC

Post box

Stamp machine

WC

Car rental

Tour operators

① 

Hotel bookings

Flight arrivals indicator

Tour operators

Meeting point

Entrance to trains British Rail

Barclays Bank cash dispensers

Moving walkway to and from car parks, coaches, hotel courtesy coaches and north entrance

# The Estate Agent

Here are 8 properties for sale. Match the picture with the description and then rewrite the items in *italics* as you would expect to see them in an estate agent's window. Remember that you want to sell them so you have to make them sound as good as possible!

1  *Big* bungalow *close to bus stop*.
2  *Small* terraced house *that looks unusual*.
3  *An old-fashioned* cottage in *the countryside*.
4  *Top floor* apartment in *expensive* area.
5  *Shop* in a *rather quiet* area of town.
6  A *separate* house in a *popular* area.
7  *Independent* second floor flat in a *modern house in town*.
8  Holiday villa with a *nice* view near *shopping centre* and *sports complex* with *swimming pool*.

For example: 1 = Picture G and would be written as:
Spacious bungalow convenient for public transport.

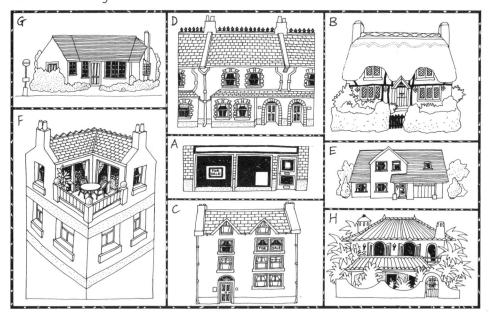

commercial premises    unspoilt rural surroundings    panoramic    detached
converted town-house    convenient for public transport    of character    select
spacious    sought-after    all major amenities    self-contained    compact
a listed period    fast-growing    penthouse

    Heinemann International

# DOMINOES 2

Now play a game with these 17 dominoes to find words connected with going on holiday. If you play correctly you'll use all the dominoes.

For example:

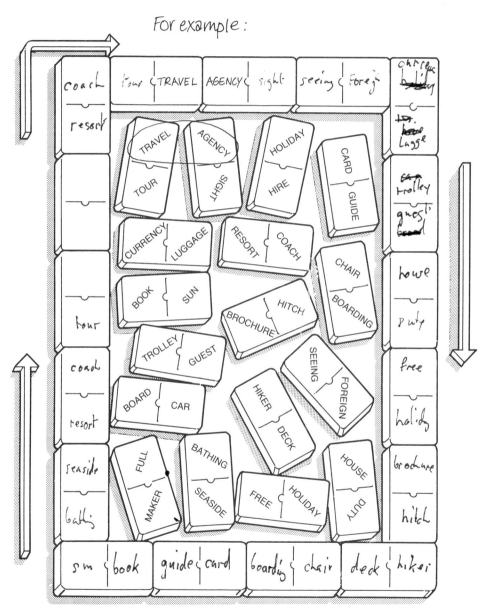

# The British Way of Life

What do British people mean when they talk about the following?
Circle the correct answer.

*For example:*

**1** *The Union Jack* is
**a** the central chamber of the Houses of Parliament
**(b)** the flag of Great Britain and Northern Ireland
**c** the most valuable prize in a game

**2** An *M.P.* is
**a** a Member of the Police
**b** a Master of Political Science
**c** a Member of Parliament

**3** A *public school* is
**a** a state school
**b** a private school
**c** a religious school

**4** *New Scotland Yard* is
**a** the material used to make bagpipes
**b** the headquarters of the police in London
**c** a measurement of length

**5** A *zebra crossing* is
**a** a place to cross the road safely
**b** a television screen for black and white reception
**c** a design of two bones used on flags

**6** A *Tory* is
**a** a numbered ticket in a lottery
**b** a coin worth £2
**c** a supporter of the Conservative Party

**7** A *Building Society* is
**a** an organization that preserves historic buildings
**b** a business which lends money to buy a house or flat
**c** a house joined to the house next door

**8** *G.C.S.E.* is
**a** a system of examinations for school children
**b** the national gas and electricity boards
**c** the highest award given by the Queen for bravery

**9** A *Trade Union* is
**a** an import export agreement
**b** an exhibition of commercial products
**c** an organization of workers

**10** A *public convenience* is
**a** a charity
**b** a public toilet
**c** a pub

# Clothing and Accessories

This crossword has been completed without any consonants. Fill in the missing letters using as clues the articles of clothing, parts of clothing and footwear and accessories that are illustrated. Number each one to show its position in the crossword.

For example:

# The Quarterly

Below you see details of Peter Williams's quarterly bank statement, showing his expenditure and receipts over the last three months. Complete this by writing + if the money is coming into his account and − if the money is going out, and by filling in the balance each time.

| ITEM | AMOUNT IN £ | IN (+) | OUT (−) | BALANCE |
|---|---|---|---|---|
| Salary | 4000 | + | | 4000 |
| Rent for last quarter | 1100 | | − | 2900 |
| Direct Debit (Telecom) | 90 | | | |
| School Fees | 375 | | | |
| Insurance Premium | 120 | | | |
| Road Tax | 55 | | | |
| Family Allowances | 75 | | | |
| Overtime | 45 | | | |
| Annual Subscription D.I.Y. News | 35 | | | |
| T.V. Licence Fee | 55 | | | |
| Interest from Savings Account | 65 | | | |
| Charity Donation | 30 | | | |
| Garage Bill for Car Repairs | 350 | | | |
| Membership Fee Photography Circle | 55 | | | |
| Credit Card Withdrawal | 400 | | | |
| Purchase Travellers' Cheques | 500 | | | |
| Answer Phone Rental | 90 | | | |
| Settlement of Quarterly Account "Maximarket" | 350 | | | |
| Parking Fines | 120 | | | |
| Subscription Executive Health Plan | 110 | | | |
| Mail Order (curtains) | 65 | | | |
| Credit Card Debit | 267 | | | |

If you are correct, the final balance will show the age of majority in Britain. Each of these short extracts refers to one of the items on the account. Can you match them?

For example: extract 1 refers to the item Charity Donation

1
**If you believe in crisis prevention, there is a simple, powerful way to react – become a sponsor. Our sponsorship rate is £7.00 a month or you can always send a higher or lower amount to be used where the need is greatest.**

2
*You can order with the full knowledge and certainty that they will offer you the same quality and value as your Stretch Covers and will co-ordinate your living room beautifully. And for a money-saving discount price that we believe is unbeatable!*

# Account

**3**

The Bank will normally send a monthly statement to the Principal Cardholder who will pay within 25 days following the statement, not less than 5% of the amount shown. The Cardholder will also pay immediately any outstanding excess over the Credit Limit.

**4**

If, on the other hand, the waiting list is less than 8 weeks, our plan will pay you £22 for every night you stay in an NHS hospital. You can use this money as you wish.

You should now know enough about Peter Williams to be able to answer the following questions:

|  | YES | NO | REASON |
|---|---|---|---|
| 1   He is out of work at the moment. |  | X | *He receives a salary.* |
| 2   He has children. |  |  |  |
| 3   He lives in rented accommodation. |  |  |  |
| 4   He does his own car repairs. |  |  |  |
| 5   He receives money from the state. |  |  |  |
| 6   He has at least 2 different accounts. |  |  |  |
| 7   He has had his credit card taken away. |  |  |  |
| 8   He will probably be going abroad soon. |  |  |  |
| 9   He is in debt to the telephone company. |  |  |  |
| 10   He gets regular copies of a handyman's magazine. |  |  |  |
| 11   His TV is illegal. |  |  |  |
| 12   He rents a garage. |  |  |  |

# A Picture Postcard

This postcard has been written in pictures not words. Can you read it?

© Howard-Williams/Herd 1989

Heinemann International

# On the Road

There are many specialized words connected with roads and transport. Read the clues and cross out the correct word or words **on the road each time**.

**A   WHAT IS IT?**   *For example:*

1   It's under your right foot. *(brake)*
2   A problem when it's flat.
3   Part of a car also worn on the foot.
4   Something horrible to find on your windscreen.
5   Where you carry a bike on a car.
6   The fifth tyre.
7   Part of a car also found on the head of a rhinocerous.

**B   DOUBLES**

Find the second part:

8   traffic _____

9   windscreen _____

10   number _____

11   steering _____

12   zebra _____

13   dual _____

14   head _____

15   exhaust _____

**C   ROAD SIGNS**

Identify these road signs:

16      17      18      19      20      21      22      23

*lights   no through road   pipe   plate   wheel*
*steep hill downwards   no overtaking   Parking ticket*
*horn   tyre   highway   carriageway*
*start of motorway   no motor vehicles   roof-rack   spare tyre*
*brake   uneven road   boot   crossing*
*code   slippery road   wipers   side road*
*warden*

So now you should be left with 2 words. If you are correct you'll see the name of a little book that's a bestseller! *The* . . . . . . . . . . . . . . . .

# Two's Company

Here are 16 compound adjectives with the two parts mixed up. The pictures illustrate 16 nouns with which they are frequently associated.
Start with the picture, match it with the noun from column C and then choose the correct adjective, taking the first part from column A and the second part from column B.

For example:
Absent-minded professor

| A | B | C |
|---|---|---|
| man | leaf | children |
| high | aid | lens |
| three | up | tiger |
| absent | minded | team |
| wide | headed | ice-cream |
| oil | privileged | man |
| open | necked | flats |
| record | flavoured | cinema |
| loose | eating | countries |
| chocolate | rise | room |
| drive | in | professor |
| pick | producing | truck |
| twin | dimensional | kit |
| bald | bedded | picture |
| under | breaking | notebook |
| first | angle | shirt |

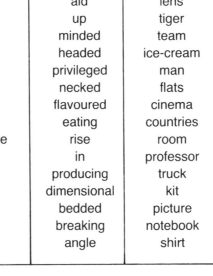

# Sayings

If you match each line of boxes at the top of the page with a line of boxes at the bottom of the page you'll be able to read 4 well known English proverbs, Work out what they are, then match them with the correct explanation (A, B, C or D).

For example: 1 + 7 = Every cloud has a silver lining. (Explanation D)

**1** | E | E | Y | | C | O | D | H | S | | A | | S | L | E | | | I | | I | | G | **1**

**2** | O | E | | S | A | L | W | | D | E | | N | T | M | K | | A | | S | M | E | **2**

**3** | I | | S | N | | U | E | | C | Y | N | | O | E | | S | | I | T | | M | L | **3**

**4** | D | N | | L | O | | A | G | F | | H | R | E | | I | | T | E | | M | U | H | **4**

---

**5** | N | | W | L | O | | O | S | | O | | A | E | | | U | M | R | **5**

**6** | O | T | | O | K | | | I | T | | O | S | | N | | H | | O | T | **6**

**7** | V | R | | L | U | | A | | | I | V | R | L | | N | N | **7**

**8** | T | | O | S | | R | I | G | V | R | | P | L | | I | K | **8**

**A** *Don't worry about something bad that has happened if there's nothing you can do about it.*

**B** You shouldn't criticise something you've had for nothing.

**C** Don't think that one hopeful sign means that everything is going to go right.

**D** However bad something may appear, something good can always come out of it.

Heinemann International **33**

# Mind and

At this party all the guests are talking about their feelings by using expressions connected with the body.

Find somebody expressing:
**A** wonder  **B** disbelief  **C** surprise  **D** disgust  **E** weakness  **F** terror
**G** rage  **H** disagreement  **I** panic  **J** irritation  **K** strong emotion
**L** relief  **M** obstinacy  **N** grief  **O** dismay  **P** calmness  **Q** sympathy
**R** discretion  **S** anticipation  **T** nervousness

For example:
A wonder = 1
It took my breath away.

          Heinemann International

# Body

# Train of thought

Work out the link between the first two words and then find a similar link to finish the sentence.

*For example :*

1. *Clock* is to *tick* as dog is to:
   **a** roar **b** grunt **ⓒ** growl **d** buzz

2. *Man* is to *chap* as *child* is to:
   **a** friend **b** pal **c** kid **d** guy

3. *Blunt* is to *sharpen* as *loose* is to:
   **a** tighten **b** find **c** lengthen **d** paint

4. *Football* is to *pitch* as *running* is to:
   **a** course **b** track **c** court **d** field

5. *Students* are to *lodgings* as *prisoners* are to:
   **a** barracks **b** inns **c** hutches **d** cells

6. *Cows* are to *cattle* as *hens* are to:
   **a** crops **b** dairy **c** game **d** poultry

7. *Worthless* is to *priceless* as *wild* is to:
   **a** rare **b** tame **c** savage **d** dangerous

8. *Sight* is to *blind* as *speech* is to:
   **a** dumb **b** hearing **c** deaf **d** lame

9. *The Thames* is to *river* as *Mars* is to:
   **a** Venus **b** star **c** zodiac **d** planet

10. *Cow* is to *calf* as *cat* is to:
    **a** puppy **b** kitten **c** cub **d** colt

11. *Ireland* is to *Irish* as *Scotland* is to:
    **a** Scotch **b** Scottish **c** Gaelic **d** tartan

12. *Stubborn* is to *obstinate* as *strange* is to:
    **a** awkward **b** nasty **c** odd **d** foolish

13. *Goats* are to *herd* as *wolves* are to:
    **a** flock **b** troop **c** swarm **d** pack

14. *Novel* is to *author* as *opera* is to:
    **a** singer **b** musician **c** composer **d** conductor

     Heinemann International

# WORDBOARD 2

Now you are looking for 2 words that sound the same, but have different spellings and different meanings (eg PIECE / PEACE). The pictures will give you clues to the words to go on the top lines and the definitions at the bottom of the page will give you clues to the words to go on the bottom lines.

For example:

IMPORTANT    EXPENSIVE    AMERICAN MONEY    FED UP
CAPTURED    GOODS AT LOW PRICES    NOT MOVING
1 (MAN OR BOY)    ROADS    TWO    REFUSE    HURTING

    

# The Travel

Travel brochures use a certain style and vocabulary to make their hotels and resorts sound attractive. Look at the descriptions below and complete them using the words at the bottom of the page. Both hotels use the same 9 words.

*For example:*

## THE IMPERIAL HOTEL

(1) _Situated_ only five minutes from the Floral Square, (2) _____ the waterfront of the River Bari, a (3) _____ hotel with all (4) _____, including a (5) _____ ballroom used for all the important functions of the town. Patio gardens, rooftop restaurant serving (6) _____ dishes. Large (7) _____ bar, popular with the locals and residents makes a (8) _____ atmosphere in (9) _____ surroundings.

## THE CONTINENTAL HOTEL

Everything has been thought of to make your stay ( ) _____. All bedrooms have private ( ) _____ and look out onto a ( ) _____ courtyard. (1) _Situated_ a few steps from the east canal, this hotel enjoys ( ) _____ views of the port and out to sea. The residents can enjoy, completely free of charge, the ( ) _____ Island Club ( ) _____ the hotel, which consists of a bar and ballroom. The ( ) _____ gamesroom is supervised by ( ) _____ and efficient staff.

well run    traditional    comfortable    close to    spectacular    luxury
friendly    facilities    ~~situated~~

# Brochure

Both these descriptions of beauty spots also have 9 words missing which are the same. Find the pairs by fitting the letters together to make the words.

*For example: 1 = features*

### Cirali

The distinctive (**1**) _f_a_u_e_ of Cirali are its much-valued historical, architectural and artistic treasures. Built around a steep hill (**2**) _s_r_o_n_e_ by undulating valleys, Cirali occupies a (**3**) _r_m_r_a_l_ position in the heart of the countryside. The (**4**) _r_n_e____ of monuments to be seen is impressive—much is (**5**) _p_e_e_v_d of all the ages, a true history book of the past (**6**) _L_n_e____ to our present civilisation. Modern (**7**) _d_v_l_p_e_t has not interfered with the ancient town of steep streets and (**8**) _a_l_y_a_s_, just as the (**9**) _v_n_y_r_s have not interfered with the fields of wheat.

### Lasyp

Lasyp is a ( ) _e_a_k_b_e mediaeval town untouched by recent ( ) _e_e_o_m_n_ ( ) _u_r_u_d_d by rocky mountains it is sometimes called 'The City of Silence'. The narrow, picturesque streets are ( ) _i_k_d____ by winding ( ) _L_e_w_y_. The town hall, with its well- ( ) _r_S_r_e_ tablets giving information about certain (**1**) _e_t_r_S___ of the old legal system is well worth a visit and from its bell-tower unfolds a ( ) _a_g____ of magnificient views, from ( ) _i_e_a_d_ to ancient ruins.

# GLIDOGRAM 2

Complete the Glidogram by looking at the clues. The first 12 words all contain the letters **EST** and the second 12 the letters **AL** (3 at the beginning of the word, 4 in the middle of the word and 5 at the end of the word each time).

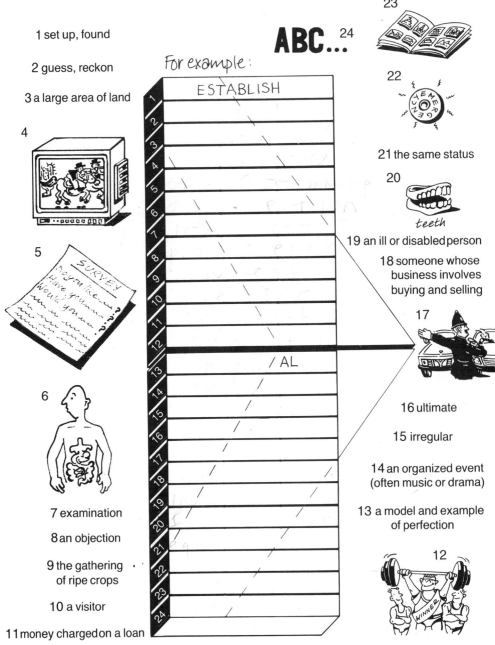

1 set up, found

2 guess, reckon

3 a large area of land

4

5

6

7 examination

8 an objection

9 the gathering of ripe crops

10 a visitor

11 money charged on a loan

For example:

ESTABLISH

ABC...

/ AL

23

24

22

21 the same status

20 teeth

19 an ill or disabled person

18 someone whose business involves buying and selling

17

16 ultimate

15 irregular

14 an organized event (often music or drama)

13 a model and example of perfection

12

# Verb Gymnastics

Find a verb that will go with the 3 words given in any one box.

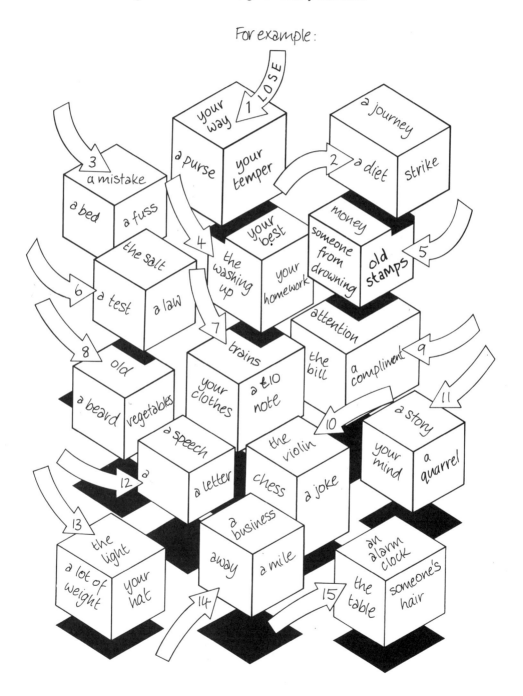

For example:

1. LOSE — your way / a purse / your temper

2. a journey / a diet / strike

3. a mistake / a bed / a fuss

4. your best / the washing up / your homework

5. money / someone from drowning / old stamps

6. the salt / a test / a law

7. trains / your clothes / a £10 note

8. old / a beard / vegetables

9. attention / the bill / a compliment

10. the violin / chess / a joke

11. a story / your mind / a quarrel

12. a speech / a / a letter

13. the light / a lot of weight / your hat

14. a business / away / a mile

15. an alarm clock / the table / someone's hair

# For Short

To save space, newspaper advertisements use a lot of abbreviations. You'll have to understand what they mean if you want to share a flat or find a job.

For the first ad. fill in the chart, saying whether the information about the ad. is correct and why or why not.

## FLAT SHARE

**Prof. F 25+ n/s to share 1 flr 3 bed flat**
**O/R Share f/f kit & bath C/H Nr Tube**
**Tel: 01 727 1296 (eves)**

*For example :*

| The person who applies to share this flat: | YES | NO | REASON |
|---|---|---|---|
| 1   must be a woman | X | | *F = female* |
| 2   can be a student | | | |
| 3   must be over 25 years old | | | |
| 4   can smoke | | | |
| 5   must share a bedroom with 3 beds in it | | | |
| 6   must share a kitchen | | | |
| 7   must provide their own kitchen equipment | | | |
| 8   will have their own bathroom | | | |
| 9   will have heating provided | | | |
| 10  will have a long walk to the Tube | | | |
| 11  will be living in London | | | |
| 12  can phone the number given at any time | | | |

For the ad. below, put the missing abbreviations into their correct place.

C.V.　　ref.　　c/o　　Ext.　　p.a.　　Sec.　　Tel.　　L.V.

## SITUATIONS VACANT

Firm of local solicitors requires       /P.A.
£12,000      , benefits include      &
season ticket.      0897-678332      225
or write with full      to P.O. Box 770,
          The Daily News. Please quote      SW/198.

# Verb Vertigo 2

No more fear of heights! Climb the phrasal verb ladder once more. The two verbs share the same three prepositions or adverbs. The words and pictures beside each group will help you to find the answers.

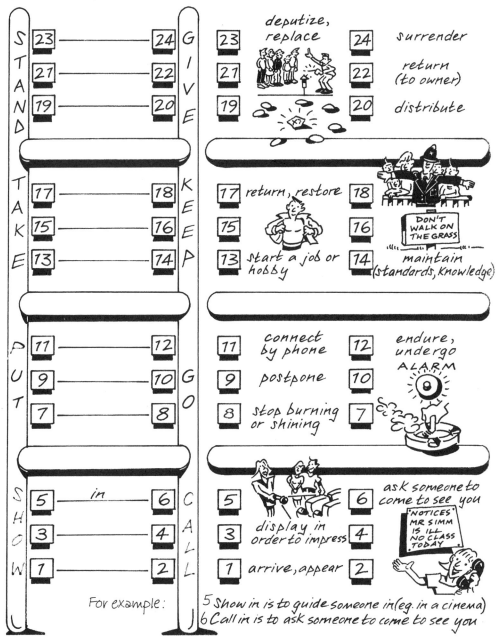

**STAND** | **GIVE**
23 — 24
21 — 22
19 — 20

23 deputize, replace
24 surrender
21
22 return (to owner)
19
20 distribute

**TAKE** | **KEEP**
17 — 18
15 — 16
13 — 14

17 return, restore
18
15
16
13 start a job or hobby
14 maintain (standards, knowledge)

**PUT** | **GO**
11 — 12
9 — 10
7 — 8

11 connect by phone
12 endure, undergo
9 postpone
10
8 stop burning or shining
7

**SHOW** | **CALL**
5 — in — 6
3 — 4
1 — 2

5
6 ask someone to come to see you
3 display in order to impress
4
1 arrive, appear
2

For example:

5 Show in is to guide someone in (eg. in a cinema)
6 Call in is to ask someone to come to see you

© Howard-Williams/Herd 1989

# Hazards in

Each part of the house has its own hazard areas. Here is a very dangerous kitchen. Look at the list of dangers below and mark each one in the picture with the corresponding letter.

| | | | |
|---|---|---|---|
| **A** | alcohol left out | **F** | hot dish on edge of worktop |
| **B** | long electric cable | **G** | spillages on floor |
| **C** | open tin | **H** | children unattended |
| **D** | sharp instruments | **I** | toxic cleaning agents lying around |
| **E** | pan handles turned outwards | **J** | matches within reach of children |

 Heinemann International

# the Home

Now look at the rest of the house and the safety precautions recommended for each area. Can you fill in the blanks with the words at the bottom of the page?

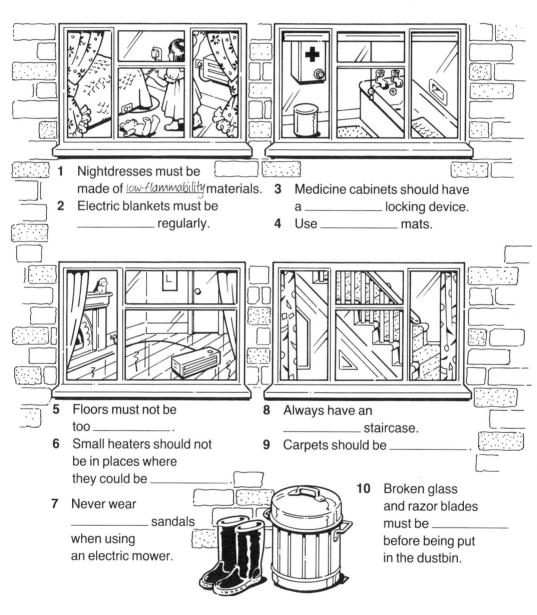

1  Nightdresses must be made of _low-flammability_ materials.
2  Electric blankets must be _____ regularly.

3  Medicine cabinets should have a _____ locking device.
4  Use _____ mats.

5  Floors must not be too _____.
6  Small heaters should not be in places where they could be _____.
7  Never wear _____ sandals when using an electric mower.

8  Always have an _____ staircase.
9  Carpets should be _____.

10  Broken glass and razor blades must be _____ before being put in the dustbin.

firmly attached    child-resistant    obstacle-free    highly polished    checked
low-flammability    rubber    open-toed    knocked over    well wrapped-up

# *Reflection*

Let's reflect on the beginnings and endings of words. The 4 words in each of the top 10 boxes can have the same prefix or suffix. Find out what it is and then check your answers in the back of the book. Sometimes you may have to change the spelling slightly.

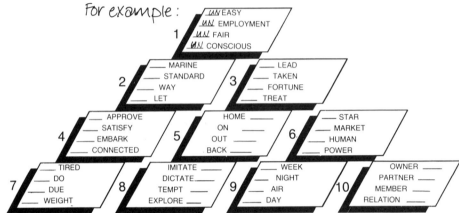

*For example:*

**1**
- *UN* EASY
- *UN* EMPLOYMENT
- *UN* FAIR
- *UN* CONSCIOUS

**2**
- ___ MARINE
- ___ STANDARD
- ___ WAY
- ___ LET

**3**
- ___ LEAD
- ___ TAKEN
- ___ FORTUNE
- ___ TREAT

**4**
- ___ APPROVE
- ___ SATISFY
- ___ EMBARK
- ___ CONNECTED

**5**
- HOME ___
- ON ___
- OUT ___
- BACK ___

**6**
- ___ STAR
- ___ MARKET
- ___ HUMAN
- ___ POWER

**7**
- ___ TIRED
- ___ DO
- ___ DUE
- ___ WEIGHT

**8**
- IMITATE ___
- DICTATE ___
- TEMPT ___
- EXPLORE ___

**9**
- ___ WEEK
- ___ NIGHT
- ___ AIR
- ___ DAY

**10**
- OWNER ___
- PARTNER ___
- MEMBER ___
- RELATION ___

Now you are ready to go on. The 4 words in each of the bottom 10 boxes go with one of the answers from the corresponding box above. *For example:* all the words in box 1 go with the word UNFAIR (unfair dismissal, unfair advantage, unfair treatment, unfair comment).

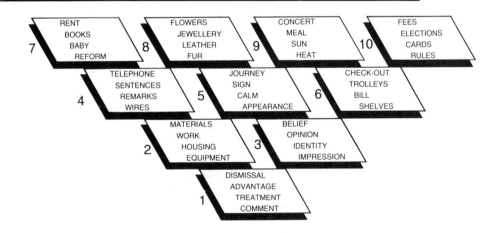

**7**
- RENT
- BOOKS
- BABY
- REFORM

**8**
- FLOWERS
- JEWELLERY
- LEATHER
- FUR

**9**
- CONCERT
- MEAL
- SUN
- HEAT

**10**
- FEES
- ELECTIONS
- CARDS
- RULES

**4**
- TELEPHONE
- SENTENCES
- REMARKS
- WIRES

**5**
- JOURNEY
- SIGN
- CALM
- APPEARANCE

**6**
- CHECK-OUT
- TROLLEYS
- BILL
- SHELVES

**2**
- MATERIALS
- WORK
- HOUSING
- EQUIPMENT

**3**
- BELIEF
- OPINION
- IDENTITY
- IMPRESSION

**1**
- DISMISSAL
- ADVANTAGE
- TREATMENT
- COMMENT

# ANSWERS

## FOOD FOR THOUGHT Page 1

1 bread  2 meat  3 sauce  4 coffee  5 fish
6 vegetable curry  7 wine  8 fruit
A strong, milky, sweet, refreshing, weak, iced
B hard, strong, ripe, mild, tasty, crumbly
C still, fizzy, sweet, sparkling, refreshing, iced

## FOUR OF A KIND Page 2

1 box  2 house  3 machine  4 car 5 board
6 paper  7 card 8 glasses  9 room  10 bag
11 coat  12 pot  13 line  14 horse 15 book
16 party  17 name 18 table  19 end
20 course

## WORD PERFECT Page 3

1 appointment  2 loose  3 advertisement
4 row  5 souvenir  6 employee  7 take
8 information  9 interval  10 earn  11 angle
12 sensitive  13 melt  14 economical
15 clothes  16 quiet  17 warning  18 lose
19 win  20 angel

## WHAT'S ON TV TONIGHT?
### Page 4

1 news  2 panel game  3 music
4 party political broadcast  5 variety show
6 late night thriller  7 educational  8 sports
9 cartoons  10 documentary  11 quiz show
12 religious broadcast

5 people who appear on the screen: announcer, interviewer, newscaster, presenter, commentator
4 people who work behind the scenes: cameraman, director, designer, producer
3 parts of a television: serial, buttons, plug
2 slang words for television: telly, the box
1 word for those who watch: viewers

## LEISURE AND PLEASURE
### Page 6

1 knitting  2 antiques  3 pottery  4 darts
5 chess  6 pets  7 drama  8 models
9 bridge  10 fashion  11 cookery
12 aerobics

| a | e | r | o | b | i | c | s | l | u | i |
|---|---|---|---|---|---|---|---|---|---|---|
| w | l | a | k | m | o | d | e | l | s | g |
| u | d | o | n | g | h | c | h | e | s | s |
| f | e | h | i | d | o | f | u | t | c | y |
| a | r | d | t | a | m | q | a | d | r | b |
| s | t | r | t | r | i | x | t | e | l | r |
| h | s | a | i | t | u | s | k | y | p | i |
| i | b | m | n | s | n | o | l | j | e | d |
| o | r | a | g | e | o | z | d | s | t | g |
| n | t | q | h | c | s | a | u | p | s | e |
| y | d | e | t | p | o | t | t | e | r | y |

## TREASURE HUNT Page 7

1 G  2 O  3 L  4 D  5 A  6 N  7 D  8 D
9 I  10 A  11 M  12 O  13 N  14 D  15 S
The treasure is in *Square T* (in the nest).
The treasure is *GOLD AND DIAMONDS*

## DOMINOES 1 Page 8

1 deep freeze  2 carving knife  3 dishwasher
4 microwave  5 teatowel  6 saucepan
7 bottle-opener  8 napkin  9 tablecloth
10 cupboard  11 nutcracker  12 tin-opener
13 tablespoon  14 corkscrew  15 teaspoon
16 potato-peeler  17 frying-pan

# THE ANIMAL KINGDOM Page 9

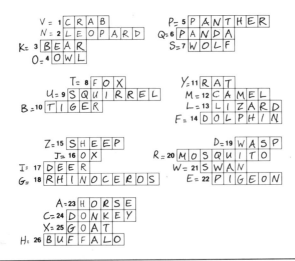

V = 1 | C R A B
N = 2 | L E O P A R D
K = 3 | B E A R
O = 4 | O W L

P = 5 | P A N T H E R
Q = 6 | P A N D A
S = 7 | W O L F

T = 8 | F O X
U = 9 | S Q U I R R E L
B = 10 | T I G E R

Y = 11 | R A T
M = 12 | C A M E L
L = 13 | L I Z A R D
F = 14 | D O L P H I N

Z = 15 | S H E E P
J = 16 | O X
I = 17 | D E E R
G = 18 | R H I N O C E R O S

D = 19 | W A S P
R = 20 | M O S Q U I T O
W = 21 | S W A N
E = 22 | P I G E O N

A = 23 | H O R S E
C = 24 | D O N K E Y
X = 25 | G O A T
H = 26 | B U F F A L O

# CRIME AND PUNISHMENT
## Page 10

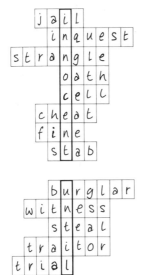

jail
inquest
strangle
oath
cell
cheat
fine
stab

burglar
witness
steal
traitor
trial

prison
arrest
rob
verdict
safe
offence

smuggle
court
bribe
plead
theft
jury

And the belief is: INNOCENT UNTIL PROVEN GUILTY

# GLIDOGRAM ONE Page 12

1 orchestra  2 orderly  3 oral  4 horizon
5 sorrow  6 sore  7 border  8 error
9 interior  10 tailor  11 superior
12 conductor  13 decent  14 permanent
15 scent  16 comment  17 violent
18 intent  19 mental  20 mention
21 entertain 22 dentist  23 entry/entrance
24 enterprise

# THE GOOD COMPANIONS
## Page 13

1 G  2 N  3 M  4 L  5 C  6 D  7 I  8 B
9 K  10 H  11 F  12 J  13 A  14 E

## FAMILY GATHERINGS Page 14

1 (insect) snail  2 (reptile) frog
3 (fish) whale  4 (material) ribbon
5 (ship) raft  6 (tree) log  7 (fruit) seed
8 (dessert) porridge  9 (island) America

10 (virtue) envy  11 (vehicle) launch
12 (china) napkin  13 (sense) thought
14 (vice) patience  15 (metal) coal

## WORDBOARD I Page 15

| 1 | MIND<br>TO LOOK AFTER<br>TO OBJECT TO | 2 | COACH<br>CARRIAGE<br>A SPORTS TRAINER | 3 | FAIR<br>BLONDE<br>AN EXHIBITION | 4 | STAGE<br>A PLATFORM IN A THEATRE<br>A PERIOD IN A DEVELOPMENT |
|---|---|---|---|---|---|---|---|
| 5 | STATE<br>EXPRESS IN WORDS<br>A POLITICAL COMMUNITY | 6 | HARD<br>SEVERELY<br>WITH GREAT ENERGY | 7 | FINE<br>PENALTY<br>DELICATE | 8 | PATIENT<br>CALM<br>A SICK PERSON |
| 9 | HAND<br>PASS<br>A POINTER ON A CLOCK | 10 | STILL<br>QUIET<br>NOT SPARKLING | 11 | STAND<br>ENDURE<br>A SMALL STALL | 12 | CASE<br>EXAMPLE<br>A MEDICAL PROBLEM |

## SUPERTRIPS Page 16

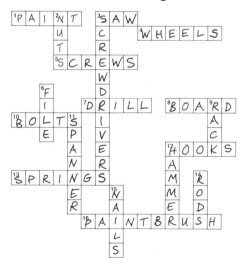

→ See No.5 Complaints

... the swimming pool was terribly dirty and I slipped on
See
No.25  the steps and now can't use my right thumb. The return
See
No.9  flight was changed at the last minute, so I missed my
connection and you gave me an aisle seat when I wanted to
See
No.13  be beside the window. And when I opened my case at home,
See
No.24  all my glass souvenirs were broken ...

A 4, 23  B 20  C 8  D 19  E 2  F 11 G 14
H 21  I 17  J 16  K 18  L 7

## DO-IT-YOURSELF Page 18

¹P A I ²N T  ³S A W
       U    C    ⁴W H E E L S
       T    R
      ⁵S C R E W S
           W
   ⁶F      D
   I      ⁷D R I L L    ⁸B O A ⁹R D
  ¹⁰B O L T ¹¹S          I        A
   E      P    I              C
   A      E              ¹²H O O K S
   N      R              A
  ¹³S P R I N G S        M    ¹⁴R
   E      ¹⁵N    M    O
   R      A              E    D
      ¹⁶P A I N T B R U S H
           L
           S

## SYLLABLE SEARCH Page 19

1 a relationship  2 a cigarette
3 an examination  4 a compliment
5 an operation  6 a competition
7 an invitation  8 a promise  9 a photograph
10 an orchestra  11 an application
12 influenza  13 a conversation  14 the violin
15 a company

## SMALL ADS Page 20

1 sun-roof grill  2 pump loudspeakers

3 sideboard tele-lens  4 plastering

organic  5 labels sun-roof  6 tele-lens

bulbs  7 playpens sideboard  8 grill

plastering  9 pedigree pump

10 loudspeakers playpens  11 organic

pedigree  12 bulbs labels

solid oak  7  free range  4  auto-focus
3  lovely temperament  11  stereo headphones
2  filing cabinets  12  self-cleaning oven
1 free estimates  8  low mileage  5  dolls  10  3-
speed  9  rakes  6

## VERB VERTIGO Page 21

1 Break out  2 Cut out  3 Break down
4 Cut down  5 Break up  6 Cut up  7 Set out
8 Look out  9 Set in  10 Look in  11 Set up
12 Look up  13 Turn out  14 Bring out
15 Turn off  16 Bring off  17 Turn up
18 Bring up  19 Get out  20 Come out
21 Get down  22 Come down  23 Get on
24 Come on

## GATWICK AIRPORT Page 22

1 Travel to and from the Airport: A 23 trunk road, fully signposted
2 Flight Departures: gate number, X-ray machines, check-in, boarding card, security search
3 Duty and Tax Free Shopping: allowances, brand names, reclaiming V.A.T.
4 Refreshments: pastries, real ale, take away, beverages
5 Flight Arrivals: free trolleys, landing card, red channel
6 Facilities at the Airport: chapel, wheelchair users, coinless cardphones (free trolleys)

### INTERNATIONAL FLIGHT ARRIVALS
### 2nd FLOOR OF TERMINAL

*What happened to the secret documents?*
Mr. X had an accomplice waiting for him at the airport and carrying an identical parcel. This accomplice was the passer-by who pretended to help him with the slot machine (which was, of course, not jammed at all). The passer-by was heading for the Post Office counter, so it seemed perfectly natural that she should be carrying a parcel too. They had timed this to coincide with the mail collection and under cover of the opening of the post box etc they were able to exchange parcels. The accomplice then took the parcel containing the secret documents to the counter and posted it. Mr. X, now carrying the empty parcel, then lead the police away from the Post Office and out of the Airport.

However *you* may, of course, have other ideas!

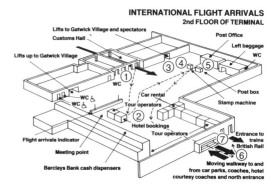

**INTERNATIONAL FLIGHT ARRIVALS**
2nd FLOOR OF TERMINAL

## THE ESTATE AGENT Page 24

1 G *Spacious* bungalow *convenient for public transport*
2 D *Compact* terraced house *of character*
3 B A *listed period* cottage in *unspoilt rural surroundings*
4 F *Penthouse* apartment in *select* area
5 A *Commercial premises* in a *fast-growing* area of town
6 E A *detached* house in a *sought after* area
7 C *Self-contained* second floor flat in a *converted town-house*
8 H Holiday villa with a *panoramic* view near *all major amenities*

## DOMINOES 2 Page 25

1 TRAVEL AGENCY   2 SIGHTSEEING
3 FOREIGN CURRENCY
4 LUGGAGE TROLLEY   5 GUEST HOUSE
6 DUTY FREE   7 HOLIDAY MAKER
8 FULL BOARD   9 CAR HIRE
10 HOLIDAY BROCHURE   11 HITCHHIKER
12 DECK CHAIR   13 BOARDING CARD
14 GUIDE BOOK   15 SUNBATHING
16 SEASIDE RESORT   17 COACH TOUR

## THE BRITISH WAY OF LIFE
### Page 26

1 b  2 c  3 b  4 b  5 a  6 c  7 b  8 a
9 c  10 b

## CLOTHING AND ACCESSORIES Page 27

# THE QUARTERLY ACCOUNT
## Page 28

Salary + Rent − Direct Debit − School fees − Insurance Premium − Road tax − Family Allowances + Overtime + DIY News subscription − TV Licence fee − Interest from savings account + Charity donation − Garage bill − Membership fee Photography Circle − Credit card withdrawal − Purchase traveller's cheques − Maximarket − Parking fines −

Health Plan Subscription − Mail Order − Credit Card Account Debit − And the balance is £18. 18 is the age of majority in Britain.

1 Charity Donation
2 Mail Order (curtains)
3 Credit Card  Account Debit
4 Subscription Executive  Health Plan

| | YES | NO | |
|---|---|---|---|
| 1 | | X | He receives a salary. |
| 2 | X | | He receives family allowance and pays school fees. |
| 3 | X | | He is paying rent. |
| 4 | | X | He has his car repaired at a garage and has paid a bill. |
| 5 | X | | Family allowances are paid by the state. |
| 6 | X | | This account is a savings account. |
| 7 | | X | He is using it for cash withdrawal. |
| 8 | X | | He has bought traveller's cheques. |
| 9 | | X | His bill is paid automatically every quarter. |
| 10 | X | | He has a subscription to Do-It-Yourself for a year. |
| 11 | | X | He has paid the licence fee. |
| 12 | | X | He pays a lot of fines for illegal parking. |

## A PICTURE POSTCARD Page 30

Dear James
We are having such fun at the seaside. We go swimming and sailing every day. It would be nice if you could spend a weekend with us. Looking forward to hearing from you soon.
Love from Stephen and Miranda XX

## ON THE ROAD Page 31

1 brake  2 tyre  3 boot  4 parking ticket
5 roof-rack  6 spare tyre  7 horn  8 warden
9 wipers  10 plate  11 wheel  12 crossing
13 dual  14 lights  15 pipe  16 no motor vehicles  17 uneven road  18 no overtaking
19 no through road  20 side road  21 start of motorway  22 slippery road  23 steep hill downwards
And the title of the book is *The Highway Code*

## TWO'S COMPANY Page 32

1 absent-minded professor  2 twin-bedded room  3 open-necked shirt  4 three-dimensional picture  5 drive-in cinema
6 under-privileged children  7 oil-producing countries  8 wide-angle lens  9 record-breaking team  10 man-eating tiger  11 pick-up truck  .12 loose-leaf notebook  13 chocolate-flavoured ice-cream  14 high-rise flats
15 bald-headed man  16 first-aid kit

## SAYINGS Page 33

1 + 7 = **D** Every cloud has a silver lining.
2 + 5 = **C** One swallow does not make a summer
3 + 8 = **A** It's no use crying over spilt milk
4 + 6 = **B** Don't look a gift horse in the mouth

## MIND AND BODY Page 34

**A** = 1  **B** = 11  **C** = 5  **D** = 20  **E** = 17  **F** = 3
**G** = 9  **H** = 8  **I** = 6  **J** = 14  **K** = 18  **L** = 4
**M** = 19  **N** = 12  **O** = 13  **P** = 7  **Q** = 16
**R** = 15  **S** = 10  **T** = 2

## TRAIN OF THOUGHT Page 36

**1** c  **2** c  **3** a  **4** b  **5** d  **6** d  **7** b  **8** c
**9** d  **10** b  **11** b  **12** c  **13** d  **14** c

# WORDBOARD II Page 37

**1** MAIL
MALE
MAN OR BOY

**2** COURT
CAUGHT
CAPTURED

**3** SAW
SORE
HURTING

**4** STATIONERY
STATIONARY
NOT MOVING

**5** PEAR
PAIR
TWO

**6** SCENT
CENT
AMERICAN MONEY

**7** MINER
MINOR
UNIMPORTANT

**8** WAIST
WASTE
REFUSE

**9** SAIL
SALE
GOODS AT LOW PRICES

**10** ROOTS
ROUTES
ROADS

**11** BOARD
BORED
FED UP

**12** DEER
DEAR
EXPENSIVE

---

# THE TRAVEL BROCHURE Page 38

### THE IMPERIAL HOTEL

**(1)** *Situated* only five minutes from the Floral Square, **(2)** *close to* the waterfront of the River Bari, a **(3)** *luxury* hotel with all **(4)** *facilities* including a **(5)** *spectacular* ballroom used for all the important functions of the town. Patio gardens, rooftop restaurant serving **(6)** *traditional* dishes. Large **(7)** *well run* bar, popular with the locals and residents makes a **(8)** *friendly* atmosphere in **(9)** *comfortable* surroundings.

### THE CONTINENTAL HOTEL

Everything has been thought of to make your stay **(9)** *comfortable*. All bedrooms have private **(4)** *facilities* and look out onto a **(6)** *traditional* courtyard. **(1)** *Situated* a few steps from the east canal, this hotel enjoys **(5)** *spectacular* views of the port and out of sea. The residents can enjoy, completely free of charge, the **(3)** *luxury* Island Club **(2)** *close to* the hotel, which consists of a bar and ballroom. The **(8)** *well run* gamesroom is supervised by **(9)** *friendly* and efficient staff.

### Cirali

The distinctive **(1)** *features* of Cirali are its much valued historical, architectural and artistic treasures. Built around a steep hill **(2)** *surrounded* by undulating valleys, Cirali occupies a **(3)** *remarkable* position in the heart of the countryside. The **(4)** *range* of monuments to be seen is impressive — much is **(5)** *preserved* of all the ages, a true history book of the past **(6)** *linked* to our present civilisation. Modern **(7)** *development* has not interfered with the ancient town of steep streets and **(8)** *alleyways*, just as the **(9)** *vineyards* have not interfered with the fields of wheat.

### Lasyp

Lasyp is a **(3)** *remarkable* mediaeval town untouched by recent **(7)** *developments*. **(2)** *Surrounded* by rocky mountains it is sometimes called 'The City of Silence'. The narrow, picturesque streets are **(6)** *linked* by winding **(8)** *alleyways*. The town hall, with its well **(5)** *preserved* tablets giving information about certain **(1)** *features* of the old legal system is well worth a visit and from its bell-tower unfolds a **(4)** *range* of magnificent views, from **(9)** *vineyards* to ancient ruins.

---

# GLIDOGRAM 2 Page 40

**1** establish  **2** estimate  **3** estate  **4** western
**5** questionnaire  **6** digestion/intestine
**7** investigation  **8** protest  **9** harvest
**10** guest  **11** interest  **12** contest  **13** ideal
**14** festival  **15** occasional  **16** final  **17** signal
**18** dealer  **19** invalid  **20** false  **21** equality
**22** alarm  **23** album  **24** alphabet

# VERB GYMNASTICS Page 41

**1** lose  **2** go on  **3** make  **4** do  **5** save
**6** pass  **7** change  **8** grow  **9** pay  **10** play
**11** make up  **12** deliver  **13** put on  **14** run
**15** set

# FOR SHORT Page 42

| | YES | NO | |
|---|---|---|---|
| 1 | X | | F = female |
| 2 | | X | Prof = Professional |
| 3 | X | | 25+ |
| 4 | | X | n/s = non-smoker |
| 5 | | X | 3 bed flat = 3 bedroom flat / O/R = Own Room |
| 6 | X | | Kit = kitchen |
| 7 | | X | f/f = fully fitted |
| 8 | | X | share bath = bathroom |
| 9 | X | | c/H = Central heating |
| 10 | | X | Nr Tube = near Tube |
| 11 | X | | Tube is London Underground / 01 is for London numbers |
| 12 | | X | eves = evenings |

(i) Sec. (Secretary)  (ii) p.a. (per annum = a year)  (iii) L.V. (Luncheon Vouchers)  (iv) Tel. (Telephone)  (v) Ext. (Extension)  (vi) C.V. (Curriculum Vitae = a short written account of a person's qualifications and work experience)  (vii) $^{c}/_{o}$ (care of)  (viii) ref. (reference)

---

## VERB VERTIGO II Page 43

**1** Show up  **2** Call up  **3** Show off  **4** Call off  **5** Show in  **6** Call in  **7** Put out  **8** Go out  **9** Put off  **10** Go off  **11** Put through  **12** Go through  **13** Take up  **14** Keep up  **15** Take off  **16** Keep off  **17** Take back  **18** Keep back  **19** Stand out  **20** Give out  **21** Stand back  **22** Give back  **23** Stand in  **24** Give in

## HAZARDS IN THE HOME
### Page 44

**1** low-flammability  **2** checked  **3** child-resistant  **4** rubber  **5** highly-polished  **6** knocked over  **7** open-toed  **8** obstacle-free  **9** firmly attached  **10** well wrapped-up

## REFLECTION Page 46

**1** UN  **2** SUB  **3** MIS  **4** DIS  **5** WARD  **6** SUPER  **7** OVER  **8** ATION  **9** MID  **10** SHIP

PART TWO

**1** UNFAIR  **2** SUBSTANDARD  **3** MISTAKEN  **4** DISCONNECTED  **5** OUTWARD  **6** SUPERMARKET  **7** OVERDUE  **8** IMITATION  **9** MIDDAY  **10** MEMBERSHIP

# WORDLIST

## A

abroad  *6, 29*
absent-minded  *32*
accident  *16*
accommodation  *17*
accomplice  *23*
ache  *13*
acrylic  *14*
act  *6*
actor  *37*
admiration  *40*
advertisment  *3*
advice  *3*
aerial  *4*
aerobics  *6*
aggressive  *12, 13*
agreement  *26*
aim  *6, 12*
airport  *22*
aisle  *16*
alarm  *40*
alarm clock  *41*
album  *40*
alleyways  *39*
alligator  *14*
allocation  *16*
allowances  *22*
along  *7*
alphabet  *40*
amateur  *6*
amenities  *24*
America  *14*
amount  *27*
ancient  *39*
angel  *3*
anger  *14*
angle  *3*
animals  *16*
announcer  *5*
annual  *20*
annual subscription  *28*
ant  *14*
anticipation  *35*
antiques  *4, 6*
appear  *5, 21, 43*
applause  *6*
application  *19*
appointment  *3, 20*
apron  *6, 27*
architectural  *39*
area  *13*
argument  *13*
arrest  *10*
arrivals  *22*
arrive  *21, 43*
artistic  *39*
assembly line  *2*
athletics  *4*
attempts  *23*
attention  *41*
Australia  *14*
author  *36*
auto-focus  *20*
award  *26*
away  *41*
awfully  *1*
awkward  *36*

## B

baby  *41*

backward  *46*
bag  *2*
baggage  *16*
bagpipes  *26*
balance  *16, 28*
bald-headed  *32*
ballroom  *38*
bank statement  *28*
bargain  *4, 20*
bark  *15*
barn  *7*
barracks  *36*
bars  *18*
basket  *20*
beak  *9*
bear  *9*
beard  *41*
beat  *4*
beauty  *6*
beauty spot  *26*
bedside table  *2*
bee  *14*
beetle  *14*
beige  *20*
bell-tower  *39*
belt  *27*
bench  *7*
benefit  *16, 42*
best-selling  *41*
beverages  *22*
bicycle  *20*
bill  *41*
billiard table  *2*
birdbath  *7*
birthday party  *2*
bishop  *6*
bitch  *20*
bitter  *1*
blade  *13*
blanket  *45*
blind  *36*
blonde  *15*
blunt  *36*
board  *2, 18, 37*
boarding card  *24*
boat  *15*
body  *6*
bodywork  *20*
boil  *6*
bolts  *18*
booking  *16*
boot  *31*
border  *12*
bored  *37*
bottle-opener  *7*
bows (n)  *27*
bow (v)  *6*
box  *2, 5*
brake  *31*
brand name  *2, 22*
bravery  *14, 26*
bread  *1*
break down  *21*
break into  *19*
break off  *19*
break out  *21*
break up  *21*
bribe  *9*
bridge  *6*
bright  *13*
bring off  *21*
bring out  *21*

bring up  *21*
broadcast  *5*
buffalo  *9*
bulbs  *20*
bungalow  *24*
burglar  *10*
bushes  *7*
business  *41*
butterfly  *14*
buttons  *5*
buzz  *36*

## C

cab  *14*
cabinet  *20*
cake  *6*
calculator  *20*
calf  *36*
call in  *43*
call off  *43*
call up  *43*
calm  *15*
camel  *9*
camera  *20*
cameraman  *5*
canal  *38*
cancel  *16*
cancellation  *16*
capture  *37*
card  *2*
cardholder  *29*
cardigan  *6*
cards  *6*
card table  *2*
care  *16*
careful  *20*
careless  *45*
care of  *42*
car hire  *24*
carriage  *15, 16*
carrier bag  *2*
carrycot  *20*
carthorse  *2*
cartoons  *5*
carving knife  *7*
case  *15, 20*
cassette  *20*
castle  *6*
cats  *6*
carthorse  *2*
cell  *10, 36*
cent  *37*
centimes  *39*
challenge  *4*
champion  *24*
championship  *6*
change  *6, 41*
channel  *4*
chap  *35*
chapel  *22*
charge  *17*
charity  *26*
cheat  *10*
check  *6*
check-in  *22*
cheese  *1*
cheque book  *2*
chess  *6, 41*
chestnut  *14*
child-resistant  *44*
chimney  *20*

china  *6, 14*
chocolate-flavoured  *32*
Christmas  *17*
cigarette ends  *2*
civilization  *39*
classroom  *2*
classical  *6*
claw  *9*
clay  *6*
clean out  *44*
clear  *20*
clip-on  *20*
clock  *4, 15*
cloth  *44*
clothes  *41*
clothes line  *2*
clothing  *6*
cloud  *33*
clubs  *6*
coach  *14, 15*
coach park  *23*
coach tour  *24*
coal  *14*
cod  *14*
coffee  *1*
coin  *26*
collar  *27*
collect  *6*
collie  *20*
colt  *36*
come down  *21*
come on  *21*
come out  *21*
comfortable  *38*
comment  *12, 46*
commentator  *5*
commercial  *26*
commercial premises  *24*
community  *4, 15*
compact  *24*
compact disc player  *20*
company  *6, 12, 19*
compete  *4*
competition  *19*
complaints  *16*
compliment  *19, 41*
composer  *36*
condition  *20*
conditions  *16*
conduct  *19*
conductor  *12, 36*
connect  *43*
connection  *16*
Conservative Party  *26*
contest  *40*
convenient  *24*
converted  *24*
conversation  *19*
cooker  *20*
cookery  *6*
co-ordinate  *29*
copper  *14*
corkscrew  *8*
correspondence course  *2*
costumes  *6*
cottage  *24*
council  *26*
counter  *23*
countryside  *24, 39*
course  *36*
court  *10, 36*
courtyard  *38*